THE SCIENCE OF HAPPINESS

BOOST MENTAL WELL-BEING, OVERCOME STRESS, CULTIVATE POSITIVE HABITS – UNLOCK LASTING FULFILLMENT

PREM SAGAR SUNCHU

YOUR FREE GIFT !!

As a token of my thanks for taking out time to read my book, I would like to offer you a **Free-Gift**:

Click the Below Link and Download your **Free eBook PDF**.

"Bridges to Happiness: Stories and Wisdom from Around the World"

ABOUT THE AUTHOR

Prem Sagar Sunchu, the Accomplished Author of "The Science of Happiness"

Meet **Mr. Prem Sagar**, an ordinary soul born in the vibrant city of Secunderabad, India, where the tapestry of life weaves stories of resilience and dreams. His journey is a testament to the power of perpetual learning, where every encounter is a lesson, and every moment holds the potential for growth.

A man of many dimensions, Mr. Sagar embodies the qualities of a perpetual student, a dedicated listener, and a dreamer who gazes at the stars but keeps his feet firmly grounded. His aspirations soar high, and his relentless pursuit of them is fueled by a genuine desire to make a positive impact on those around him.

Having served as a Chief Manager in the prestigious State Bank of India, Mr. Sagar brings a wealth of experience from the world of banking. However, for him, retirement isn't a conclusion but a commencement—a reminder that life's true journey begins when one can reflect on the wisdom gained from the first innings.

In Mr. Sagar's view, retirement is not a retreat but a stepping stone to a realm of infinite possibilities. It's an opportunity to surpass the ordinary, where the canvas of life awaits new brushstrokes of creativity and purpose. For him, the "be good and do good policy" isn't just a mantra; it's a guiding principle that shapes his approach to life.

As he embraces the second innings, Mr. Sagar encourages others to view retirement not as a winding down but as a springboard to new endeavors. It's a time when accumulated wisdom meets fresh energy, and the monotony of routine gives way to the vibrancy of creativity. His belief is clear: retirement is not just a number; it's a chapter where the richness of experience meets the possibilities in abundance.

In the world of Mr. Prem Sagar, retirement is not a period of rest but a canvas waiting to be painted with the colors of newfound wisdom, creativity, and a different outlook on life.

Prem Sagar Sunchu
M.Com, LLM, Certified Independent Director (IICA)
GOI,
Author, Sole Arbitrator and Legal Consultant, Freelancer

ACKNOWLEDGEMENTS

In profound gratitude, I extend heartfelt appreciation to my amazing parents. To my caring and resilient mother, **Smt. S.L. Lakshmi**, who gracefully navigated the challenges of my father's service transfers, made countless sacrifices to bind our family together. My father, **Shri S.R. Lakshman Rao**, stands as my enduring role model—his post-retirement vibrancy, marked by a dedicated hobby of reading and writing, serves as the very foundation that propels me into the realm of authorship. A debt of gratitude is owed to my beautiful wife, **Smt. S.P. Padma Sree** is a constant source of inspiration, unwavering strength, and invaluable guidance. Balancing family responsibilities and the intricate path of an author, her presence has been the foundation of my journey.

To my handsome sons, **S.P. Gautam Sagar, S.P. Prayag Sagar**, and **S.P. Akshaj Sagar**, whose unwavering support and responsibility bear testament to the great strength they provide. Their motivation fuels my endeavors across all the diverse traits I undertake.

I owe thanks to **Mr. Som Bathla**, an **Amazon #1 Best-selling** author, for his mentorship, motivation, and guidance in the realms of **Writing, Self-Publishing, and Launching Books**. His support has been instrumental in initiating my journey as an Authorpreneur.

My Sincere thanks to **Mr. Sooraj Achar**, who is also an Amazon Bestselling Author, for his **Professional Editing,** Formatting, and Publishing support.

In acknowledging these pillars of support, I am reminded that the tapestry of my life and authorial pursuit is woven with threads of love, sacrifice, and inspiration. With profound thanks to my family, who stand as my bedrock of strength and motivation.

DEDICATION

To the guiding stars of my universe—my Parents, Grandparents, Parents-in-law, Brothers, Sisters, the cherished members of our extended Family and Friends. Their unwavering support and boundless encouragement have been the driving force behind my Author Journey.

In the tapestry of my life, each of them has woven threads of inspiration and resilience, transforming mere words into stories and dreams into realities. Their confidence in me has been a constant source of strength, propelling me forward through the path of this journey.

With heartfelt gratitude, I dedicate the pages of my work to the pillars of love and encouragement that they are, recognizing that every word I pen is a tribute to the collective spirit of our family. May this dedication reflect the depth of my appreciation for the profound impact they have had on my creative journey.

"The Science of Happiness" is my first book in the series of five books- **"The Happiness Mastery."**

CONTENTS

INTRODUCTION: UNDERSTANDING THE SCIENCE OF HAPPINESS

"Happiness is not something ready-made. It comes from your own actions." – Dalai Lama

The Pursuit of Happiness: Why It Matters More Than Ever

Happiness has been a cornerstone of human aspirations throughout history, but in today's fast-paced, hyperconnected world, its pursuit has become more complex. Studies suggest that despite rising global incomes and technological advancements, happiness levels have stagnated—or even declined—in many parts of the world. This paradox of progress raises a vital question: why are we struggling to achieve the happiness we so desperately seek?

As societal norms evolve, the definition of happiness continues to shift. Is it success? Contentment? The absence of pain? To many, happiness appears elusive because they search for it in external achievements rather than cultivating it from within. By understanding the science behind happiness, we can demystify its mechanisms and unlock sustainable pathways to joy and fulfillment.

What Is Happiness? Unpacking the Concept Through Science

Happiness is more than a fleeting emotion; it's a complex interplay of mental, physical, and social factors. Psychologists often define it using two frameworks:

1. **Hedonic Happiness**: Centered on pleasure and the avoidance of pain.

2. **Eudaimonic Happiness**: Rooted in purpose, meaning, and personal growth.

Scientific research has illuminated the neurobiology of happiness, with chemicals like dopamine, serotonin, oxytocin, and endorphins playing key roles. For example, a study published in *Nature Communications* demonstrated how sustained engagement in meaningful activities stimulates the brain's reward system, leading to long-lasting happiness. This is why experiences—such as spending time with loved ones or volunteering—often yield more satisfaction than material possessions.

The Happiness Gap: Why So Many Struggle to Feel Fulfilled

Despite increased awareness about mental health and well-being, a substantial "happiness gap" persists. Factors contributing to this include:

- **Social Comparison**: Social media exacerbates feelings of inadequacy as people compare their lives to curated highlights of others.

- **Stress and Burnout**: Chronic stress from work and life obligations erodes happiness over time.

- **Lack of Purpose**: Without clear goals or a sense of

meaning, individuals often feel adrift.

Real-Life Story: The CEO Who Lost and Found Happiness

Consider the story of Priya, a successful tech CEO in Silicon Valley. On paper, Priya had it all—wealth, accolades, and influence—but she felt deeply unfulfilled. After stepping back from her demanding role, she discovered happiness in unexpected places: mentoring young entrepreneurs and reconnecting with her artistic passions. Priya's journey illustrates how aligning life with personal values and purpose can bridge the happiness gap.

How This Book Helps: Bridging the Gap with Research and Practice

The goal of this book is to empower you with evidence-based tools to cultivate happiness, regardless of external circumstances. Unlike prescriptive advice, this approach is rooted in personalization. Happiness isn't one-size-fits-all; it's a dynamic, evolving process.

Key Topics Explored in the Book:

- **The Science Behind Habits**: Learn how daily routines shape long-term happiness.

- **Managing Stress Effectively**: Practical techniques to reduce anxiety and overwhelm.

- **Building Resilient Relationships**: How connections enhance well-being.

- **The Role of Gratitude and Mindfulness**: Unlocking joy through presence and appreciation.

Key Insights: In-Depth Analysis of Habit Formation and Happiness

1. Habits as the Building Blocks of Happiness

James Clear, author of *Atomic Habits*, posits that small changes compound over time to create transformative results. For example, consistently practicing gratitude can rewire the brain to focus on positivity, reducing stress and enhancing overall well-being.

Real-Life Story: The Digital Detox Experiment

Mark, a remote worker in his 30s, realized his excessive screen time was draining his mental energy. Inspired by digital minimalism, he began limiting social media use to 30 minutes daily and replaced evening screen time with journaling. Within weeks, Mark reported better sleep, reduced anxiety, and increased happiness. His story highlights how mindful habit changes can lead to profound improvements in quality of life.

2. Scientific Backing for Positive Habits

- A study from *The Journal of Positive Psychology* found that practicing gratitude for just five minutes a day increased happiness by 10% over six months.

- Research in *Frontiers in Psychology* showed that individuals who incorporated daily mindfulness practices experienced decreased levels of cortisol, the stress hormone.

Actionable Steps: Creating Your Happiness Routine

- **Start Small**: Begin with a single habit, such as journaling or a daily walk.

- **Track Progress**: Use habit trackers to maintain accountability.

- **Reward Yourself**: Celebrate milestones to reinforce positive behavior.

- **Adjust as Needed**: Reflect on what's working and refine your routine.

Emerging Trends in the Happiness Space

1. Digital Minimalism

The constant barrage of notifications can detract from mental well-being. Digital minimalism advocates for intentional technology use, creating space for deeper connections and creativity.

2. Habits for Remote Workers

Remote work can blur boundaries between personal and professional life, leading to burnout. Building habits like dedicated work hours, scheduled breaks, and outdoor activities can boost happiness and productivity.

Practical Tools: Interactive Elements

- **Habit Tracker Templates**: Plan and monitor your progress.

- **Mindfulness Prompts**: Daily questions to encourage reflection.

- **Gratitude Journals**: A structured space to document moments of joy.

Conclusion: Happiness Is Within Your Reach

Happiness isn't a distant destination—it's a journey shaped by daily actions and mindsets. By understanding the science of happiness and leveraging its principles, you can overcome stress, cultivate positive habits, and unlock lasting fulfillment.

Actionable Takeaways:

- Start with one small habit today—whether it's a gratitude practice or a mindful walk.

- Reflect on your values and align your actions with them.

- Embrace the idea that happiness is a skill you can develop, not a static state to achieve.

As you turn the pages of this book, let each chapter inspire you to take steps toward a life rich in joy, purpose, and connection.

Resources for Further Reading

1. Clear, James. *Atomic Habits: An Easy & Proven Way to Build Good Habits & Break Bad Ones.*

2. Seligman, Martin E.P. *Authentic Happiness: Using the New Positive Psychology to Realize Your Potential for Lasting Fulfillment.*

3. Csikszentmihalyi, Mihaly. *Flow: The Psychology of*

Optimal Experience.

4. Newport, Cal. *Digital Minimalism: Choosing a Focused Life in a Noisy World.*

5. Kabat-Zinn, Jon. *Wherever You Go, There You Are: Mindfulness Meditation in Everyday Life.*

6. Lyubomirsky, Sonja. *The How of Happiness: A New Approach to Getting the Life You Want.*

7. Brown, Brené. *The Gifts of Imperfection: Let Go of Who You Think You're Supposed to Be and Embrace Who You Are.*

8. Diener, Ed, et al. *Happiness: Unlocking the Mysteries of Psychological Wealth.*

9. Research articles from *The Journal of Positive Psychology.*

10. Articles and tools from credible sources like Harvard Health Publishing and PositivePsychology.com.

Chapter 1

The Brain and Happiness—Understanding the Neurological Pathways

"Happiness depends upon ourselves." – Aristotle

Introduction: The Brain as the Command Center of Happiness

Happiness is often seen as an abstract concept, but its roots lie in the very tangible structures of the human brain. Neuroscience has unveiled the intricate pathways and chemical messengers that govern our emotions, showing that happiness is as much about biology as it is about mindset.

Understanding these pathways is empowering: it reveals that happiness is not entirely dependent on circumstances but can be cultivated through specific actions and habits. This chapter explores the neurological foundation of happiness, providing insights into how our brain works and actionable steps to harness its potential for joy.

The Chemistry of Joy: Serotonin, Dopamine, and Endorphins Explained

Our emotions are intricately tied to the brain's chemical messengers. Known as neurotransmitters, these chemicals regulate mood, motivation, and feelings of pleasure. Three primary players in the "chemistry of joy" are:

1. Dopamine: The Motivation Molecule Dopamine is often referred to as the "reward chemical." It spikes when we anticipate a reward, reinforcing behaviors like eating, exercising, or achieving a goal. A study in *Nature Neuroscience* found that individuals with higher baseline dopamine levels were more likely to pursue long-term goals.

Actionable Tip: Set achievable micro-goals daily. Completing them triggers dopamine release, fueling motivation.

2. Serotonin: The Mood Stabilizer Serotonin is crucial for mood regulation and emotional stability. Research published in *Psychiatry Research* suggests that practices like mindfulness and exposure to sunlight naturally boost serotonin levels.

Actionable Tip: Spend at least 15 minutes daily in natural sunlight to support serotonin production.

3. Endorphins: Nature's Painkillers Released during physical activity, endorphins act as natural stress relievers, enhancing mood and reducing discomfort. The "runner's high" is a classic example of endorphin activation.

Actionable Tip: Incorporate regular aerobic exercises like jogging or cycling into your routine to boost endorphins.

Real-Life Story: The Power of Dopamine

Sarah, a middle school teacher, struggled with low energy and motivation. By adopting a daily habit of writing down three small goals each morning, she noticed a surge in her enthusiasm and productivity. This simple practice leveraged dopamine's role in reinforcing success, leading Sarah to feel more accomplished and joyful in her day-to-day life.

Neuroplasticity: Rewiring Your Brain for Positive Thinking

Neuroplasticity refers to the brain's ability to reorganize itself by forming new neural connections throughout life. This adaptability means that we can train our brain to prioritize positive thoughts and behaviors.

The Science of Neuroplasticity

Studies in *Nature Reviews Neuroscience* show that repeated thoughts and behaviors strengthen specific neural pathways, while unused ones weaken. This is the basis of the adage, "What you focus on grows."

How to Harness Neuroplasticity

- **Affirmations and Visualization**: Regularly visualizing positive outcomes reinforces optimism.

- **Mindfulness Practices**: Meditation has been shown to increase gray matter density in regions of the brain associated with happiness.

Actionable Tip: Dedicate 5–10 minutes daily to mindfulness meditation. Use guided apps like Calm or Headspace to get started.

Real-Life Story: Rebuilding Positivity After a Setback

When Tom, an entrepreneur, faced bankruptcy, he spiraled into negativity. Through cognitive behavioral therapy (CBT), he learned to challenge negative thought patterns and replace them with constructive ones. Over time, his brain adapted, and he regained confidence, eventually rebuilding a thriving business.

The Happiness Set Point: Can You Change It?

The happiness set point theory suggests that each person has a baseline level of happiness largely determined by genetics and early life experiences. While external circumstances may temporarily shift this level, the brain tends to revert to the baseline over time.

Can the Set Point Be Adjusted?

Research from *The Journal of Personality and Social Psychology* highlights that 40% of our happiness is influenced by intentional activities, such as cultivating positive habits and engaging in meaningful work. This means that while genetics play a role, we have significant control over our emotional state.

Actionable Strategies to Boost the Set Point:

- **Engage in Flow Activities**: Pursue tasks that challenge you but are enjoyable, such as painting, playing a sport, or solving puzzles.

- **Practice Altruism**: Acts of kindness have been

shown to elevate happiness levels by enhancing social connections.

The Role of Gratitude in Brain Health

Gratitude is more than a social virtue—it's a scientifically backed tool for enhancing happiness. Neuroscientific studies reveal that practicing gratitude activates the brain's reward system, fostering a positive feedback loop of joy and contentment.

Research on Gratitude

- A study in *Frontiers in Psychology* demonstrated that participants who kept a gratitude journal for just three weeks showed increased activity in the prefrontal cortex, the area of the brain responsible for decision-making and positive emotions.

- Gratitude also lowers cortisol levels, reducing stress and enhancing resilience.

Practical Ways to Cultivate Gratitude

- **Daily Journaling**: Write down three things you're

thankful for each day.

- **Gratitude Letters**: Write and share a heartfelt note of thanks to someone who has positively impacted your life.

- **Mindful Appreciation**: Take a few moments each day to savor simple pleasures, like a warm cup of coffee or a beautiful sunset.

Real-Life Story: A Gratitude Transformation

Maria, a nurse working long shifts during the pandemic, found herself overwhelmed by stress. Inspired by a friend, she started a gratitude journal, noting small victories and moments of beauty each day. This practice shifted her perspective, helping her find joy amidst chaos and deepen her sense of purpose.

Conclusion: Unlocking Happiness Through the Brain

The brain is not just a vessel for happiness—it's the architect. By understanding the roles of neurotransmitters, leveraging neuroplasticity, and embracing practices like gratitude, you can reshape your mental pathways toward sustained joy.

Actionable Takeaways

1. Incorporate habits like mindfulness and journaling to boost serotonin and dopamine naturally.

2. Embrace neuroplasticity by replacing negative thoughts with positive affirmations.

3. Use gratitude as a daily tool to foster resilience and elevate your happiness set point.

By aligning your actions with the brain's natural mechanisms, you hold the key to unlocking a happier, healthier life.

Resources for Further Reading

1. Doidge, Norman. *The Brain That Changes Itself: Stories of Personal Triumph from the Frontiers of Brain Science.*

2. Hanson, Rick. *Hardwiring Happiness: The New Brain Science of Contentment, Calm, and Confidence.*

3. Clear, James. *Atomic Habits: An Easy & Proven Way to Build Good Habits & Break Bad Ones.*

4. Kabat-Zinn, Jon. *Mindfulness for Beginners: Reclaiming the Present Moment—and Your Life.*

5. Lyubomirsky, Sonja. *The How of Happiness: A New Approach to Getting the Life You Want.*

6. Articles from *Nature Neuroscience* and *Frontiers in Psychology.*

7. Apps like Calm, Headspace, and Gratitude Journal for daily practice.

CHAPTER 2

STRESS AND MENTAL WELL-BEING— BREAKING THE CYCLE

"It's not stress that kills us; it is our reaction to it." – Hans Selye

Introduction: The Stress-Happiness Paradox

Stress is a universal experience. From juggling deadlines to managing relationships, stress often feels like an unavoidable companion in modern life. Yet, it's one of the greatest barriers to happiness and mental well-being. Chronic stress drains energy, clouds decision-making, and undermines the brain's capacity for joy.

But there's hope. By understanding how stress affects the mind and body and adopting evidence-based strategies, it's possible to disrupt the cycle and reclaim your happiness. This chapter explores the science of stress, its impact on mental well-being, and actionable techniques to foster resilience and peace.

The Science of Stress: How It Impacts Your Happiness

Stress isn't inherently bad. In small doses, it can be a powerful motivator, pushing us to meet challenges and grow. However, chronic stress—when the body remains in a prolonged state of tension—can wreak havoc on mental and physical health.

How Stress Affects the Brain

- **Cortisol Overload**: Chronic stress leads to excessive production of cortisol, the body's stress hormone. High cortisol levels have been linked to anxiety, depression, and impaired memory.

- **Happiness Chemicals Suppressed**: Stress inhibits the production of serotonin and dopamine, neurotransmitters vital for maintaining mood stability.

- **Brain Shrinkage**: Research from *Nature Neuroscience* reveals that prolonged stress can reduce the size of the prefrontal cortex, impairing decision-making and emotional regulation.

Physical Consequences of Stress

Stress is also linked to heart disease, weakened immunity, and chronic inflammation, which further affect mental well-being. A study published in *The Lancet* confirmed that stress-related illnesses significantly diminish life satisfaction and happiness.

Actionable Insight: Start by tracking your stress triggers. Identifying patterns is the first step toward breaking the cycle.

Fight, Flight, or Freeze: Managing Stress Responses Effectively

The stress response, also known as the fight, flight, or freeze mechanism, is an evolutionary survival tool. When faced with perceived danger, the body releases adrenaline and cortisol to prepare for immediate action.

Recognizing Stress Responses

1. **Fight**: Irritability, aggression, or a strong desire to confront the problem head-on.

2. **Flight**: Avoidance behaviors, procrastination, or a compulsion to escape the situation.

3. **Freeze**: Paralysis, indecision, or feeling emotionally numb.

Reframing the Stress Response

While these responses are automatic, you can train your brain to react differently through cognitive techniques:

- **Label Your Emotion**: Simply naming your stress (e

.g., "I feel overwhelmed") can activate the prefrontal cortex and reduce the intensity of the emotion.

- **Reframe the Threat**: Shift your perspective by focusing on the opportunity in the challenge, rather than the danger.

Real-Life Story: Overcoming a Freeze Moment

When Priya, a project manager, faced an unexpected layoff, her initial reaction was paralysis. With guidance from a counselor, she learned to break down her stress response, reframing it as an opportunity to explore a new career path. Over time, she not only transitioned to a new role but also discovered greater fulfillment in her work.

Mind-Body Techniques: Yoga, Meditation, and Breathing for Relief

Stress isn't just in your head—it manifests in your body. Mind-body techniques have been scientifically proven to calm the nervous system and restore balance.

Yoga: Aligning Body and Mind

Yoga combines movement, breath control, and meditation, making it a holistic stress-relief practice. Research in *The Journal of Behavioral Medicine* found that regular yoga reduces cortisol levels and enhances emotional resilience.

Actionable Tip: Try a beginner-friendly yoga flow, such as Hatha or Yin yoga, for 10–20 minutes daily to release tension.

Meditation: Quieting the Mind

Meditation promotes mindfulness, allowing you to focus on the present moment and reduce ruminative thinking. Studies from *Harvard Medical School* show that just eight weeks of meditation can increase gray matter in the brain, improving emotional regulation.

Actionable Tip: Start with guided meditations using apps like Insight Timer or Headspace. Even five minutes a day can make a difference.

Breathing Techniques: The Power of the Breath

Simple breathing exercises can activate the parasympathetic nervous system, counteracting the fight-or-flight response.

- **Box Breathing**: Inhale for 4 counts, hold for 4 counts, exhale for 4 counts, and hold for 4 counts.

- **Diaphragmatic Breathing**: Place one hand on your chest and the other on your abdomen. Breathe deeply into your belly, ensuring your abdomen rises with each inhale.

Real-Life Story: Managing Anxiety Through Meditation- After years of battling anxiety, Michael, a software engineer, found relief through mindfulness meditation. By dedicating 10 minutes each morning to meditation, he noticed a significant reduction in his stress levels and an improved ability to handle workplace challenges.

Daily Practices for a Stress-Free Life

Sustainable stress management is about incorporating small, consistent habits into your routine.

Morning Routine for Calm

1. **Start with Gratitude**: Write down three things you're grateful for.

2. **Stretch or Exercise**: Physical activity boosts endorphins, reducing stress.

3. **Mindful Planning**: Prioritize tasks to avoid feeling overwhelmed.

Midday Stress Busters

- Take short, mindful breaks to reset.

- Step outside for fresh air and sunlight to stabilize mood.

Evening Wind-Down

- Limit screen time before bed to improve sleep quality.

- Practice a bedtime ritual, such as reading or gentle stretching.

Building Resilience

1. **Cultivate a Support System**: Engage with friends, family, or support groups to share and offload stress.

2. **Develop Hobbies**: Creative pursuits like painting, gardening, or playing music can provide therapeutic relief.

Conclusion: Disrupting Stress for Happiness

Stress doesn't have to be a permanent barrier to mental well-being. By understanding the science of stress, learning to manage automatic responses, and adopting holistic practices like yoga and meditation, you can regain control over your emotions.

Actionable Takeaways

1. Recognize and label stress responses to manage them effectively.

2. Incorporate mind-body techniques into your daily routine.

3. Build stress-relief habits, starting small and scaling gradually.

Breaking the cycle of stress requires effort, but the rewards—a calmer mind, healthier body, and greater happiness—are well worth it.

Resources for Further Reading

1. McGonigal, Kelly. *The Upside of Stress: Why Stress Is Good for You, and How to Get Good at It.*

2. Kabat-Zinn, Jon. *Full Catastrophe Living: Using the Wisdom of Your Body and Mind to Face Stress, Pain, and Illness.*

3. Hanson, Rick. *Resilient: How to Grow an Unshakable Core of Calm, Strength, and Happiness.*

4. Articles from *The Lancet* and *Nature Neuroscience.*

5. Apps: Calm, Insight Timer, and Yoga with Adriene (YouTube channel).

CHAPTER 3

THE POWER OF POSITIVE HABITS—BUILDING A JOYFUL LIFE

"We are what we repeatedly do. Excellence, then, is not an act, but a habit." – Aristotle

Introduction: The Path to Joy Lies in Daily Actions

Happiness isn't a fleeting emotion but a way of life, cultivated through intentional habits. Every choice, no matter how small, either reinforces joy or undermines it.

By understanding how habits shape behavior and applying simple yet transformative techniques, you can rewire your life for positivity and purpose.

This chapter unpacks the science of habit formation, explores practical strategies like micro-habits and habit stacking, and provides actionable insights for making happiness sustainable.

The Habit Loop: Understanding and Changing Patterns

What is the Habit Loop?

According to Charles Duhigg's *The Power of Habit*, every habit operates in a three-step loop:

1. **Cue**: A trigger that initiates the habit (e.g., your phone buzzing).

2. **Routine**: The behavior itself (e.g., checking social media).

3. **Reward**: The benefit you gain (e.g., a dopamine hit from a "like").

This loop creates neurological pathways that become stronger with repetition, making habits automatic over time.

Breaking Unhelpful Patterns

To replace a negative habit with a positive one, you need to modify the loop:

- **Change the Cue**: Identify and eliminate triggers that lead to undesirable behaviors.

- **Swap the Routine**: Substitute a healthier action for the same cue.

- **Enhance the Reward**: Ensure the new habit provides immediate and meaningful gratification.

Real-Life Story: Breaking the Evening Snacking Habit

Rachel, a young professional, struggled with late-night junk food cravings, which affected her energy and mood. By identifying her cue (boredom), she replaced snacking with a 10-minute walk and rewarded herself with a relaxing herbal tea. Within weeks, the new habit became her default evening routine, leading to increased vitality and happiness.

Micro-Habits for Big Results: Simple Steps to Greater Happiness

Why Micro-Habits Work

Micro-habits are small, easily achievable actions that require minimal effort but lead to significant results over time. As B.J. Fogg explains in *Tiny Habits*, starting small reduces resistance and builds confidence, setting the stage for larger changes.

Examples of Micro-Habits for Happiness

1. **Gratitude Journal**: Write down one thing you're grateful for each day.

2. **Smile Trigger**: Smile every time you see your reflection.

3. **Mindful Minute**: Take 60 seconds to focus on your breath at a set time each day.

4. **Morning Stretch**: Begin the day with a quick stretch to boost energy and mood.

Real-Life Story: The Ripple Effect of a One-Minute Rule

Ajay, a father juggling work and family, started dedicating one minute each evening to tidying his workspace. This small action motivated him to gradually extend his efforts, creating an organized environment that reduced stress and improved his focus.

Actionable Tip: Choose one micro-habit today and commit to it for a week. Celebrate even the smallest success to build momentum.

The Role of Consistency in Well-Being

The Science of Consistency

Consistency is the cornerstone of habit formation. Neural pathways strengthen with repetition, making behaviors automatic. Research in *Psychological Science* highlights that maintaining a habit for 21–66 days is critical for it to become ingrained.

Why Consistency is Hard

Life's unpredictability often disrupts routines, leading to set-backs. The key is to start with habits that fit seamlessly into your daily life.

Strategies for Building Consistency

1. **Anchor to Existing Routines**: Pair a new habit with a well-established one. For instance, meditate right after brushing your teeth.

2. **Track Progress**: Use habit trackers or apps like Habitica to stay accountable.

3. **Start Small**: A five-minute commitment is easier to maintain than a one-hour goal.

Real-Life Example: Consistency in Physical ActivityDavid wanted to improve his fitness but struggled with regular exercise. He began with a 10-minute walk every morning after his coffee. Over months, this small habit evolved into a full workout routine, significantly enhancing his energy and happiness.

Actionable Insight: Focus on "never missing twice." If you skip a habit one day, ensure you follow through the next.

Habit Stacking: Making Happiness Practices Stick

What is Habit Stacking?

Coined by James Clear in *Atomic Habits*, habit stacking involves linking a new habit to an existing one. This leverages the brain's tendency to follow established routines, making the new habit easier to adopt.

Steps to Create a Habit Stack

1. **Identify an Anchor Habit**: Choose a daily activity, such as making coffee or brushing your teeth.

2. **Add the New Habit**: Attach the desired habit immediately before or after the anchor.

3. **Reinforce the Connection**: Celebrate your success

to solidify the habit stack.

Example Stacks for Happiness

- After brushing my teeth, I will write one positive affirmation.

- Before I eat lunch, I will take three deep breaths.

- After I finish work, I will spend 5 minutes journaling about my day.

Real-Life Story: Habit Stacking for Mindfulness

Anjali struggled with feeling present during her hectic days. She decided to pair mindfulness with her tea breaks, taking three deep breaths before each sip. Over time, this simple stack became a cherished ritual, bringing moments of calm and happiness to her routine.

Actionable Tip: Start with one habit stack this week. Choose a low-effort addition to an existing routine and gradually build on it.

Conclusion: Transforming Life, One Habit at a Time

The power of positive habits lies not in grand gestures but in the cumulative effect of small, consistent actions. By understanding the habit loop, starting with micro-habits, and leveraging strategies like habit stacking, you can create a joyful, resilient life.

Actionable Takeaways

1. Identify one habit you'd like to change and apply the habit loop framework.

2. Experiment with micro-habits that align with your happiness goals.

3. Anchor new habits to existing routines to make them stick.

Happiness isn't a destination but a practice. With the right habits, you can build a life filled with purpose, positivity, and lasting joy.

Resources for Further Reading

1. Duhigg, Charles. *The Power of Habit: Why We Do What We Do in Life and Business.*

2. Clear, James. *Atomic Habits: An Easy & Proven Way to Build Good Habits & Break Bad Ones.*

3. Fogg, B.J. *Tiny Habits: The Small Changes That Change Everything.*

4. Research Articles in *Psychological Science* and *Journal of Behavioral Medicine.*

5. Apps: Streaks, Habitica, and Fabulous for habit tracking and motivation.

By focusing on the science and application of positive habits, this chapter empowers you to craft a joyful, meaningful life one action at a time.

CHAPTER 4

RELATIONSHIPS AND HAPPINESS— CONNECTING FOR FULFILLMENT

"The quality of your life is the quality of your relationships." – Tony Robbins

Introduction: Happiness is a Shared Journey

In our pursuit of happiness, relationships play a pivotal role. Human connection is not a luxury but a necessity for well-being. Research consistently shows that strong, meaningful relationships are among the most reliable predictors of happiness and longevity.

This chapter explores the profound impact of relationships on happiness, the science behind empathy and connection, and practical strategies for navigating conflicts and fostering meaningful bonds. By mastering these skills, you can enhance your life and the lives of those around you.

The Science of Connection: Why Relationships Matter

The Biological Need for Connection

Humans are hardwired for connection. Studies in neuroscience reveal that social interactions activate the brain's reward system, releasing oxytocin—often called the "bonding hormone." This process fosters trust and emotional intimacy, both critical for happiness.

A groundbreaking 75-year study by Harvard revealed that close relationships, more than wealth or fame, keep people happy and healthy throughout their lives. Participants with strong social bonds reported better health and greater life satisfaction, even in their later years.

The Happiness Boost from Relationships

- **Shared Joy**: Celebrating achievements with loved ones amplifies happiness.

- **Stress Buffer**: Supportive relationships reduce stress, promoting resilience.

- **Sense of Purpose**: Caring for others fosters meaning and fulfillment.

Real-Life Story: The Power of Connection

Maria, a widow in her 60s, struggled with loneliness until she joined a community gardening group. The friendships she formed not only eased her isolation but also gave her a renewed sense of purpose. Her story illustrates how even small efforts to connect can transform one's life.

The Power of Empathy: Building Deeper Bonds

What is Empathy?

Empathy is the ability to understand and share another person's feelings. It fosters trust, deepens relationships, and creates a foundation for emotional intimacy.

The Science of Empathy

Research from the Greater Good Science Center shows that practicing empathy activates the brain's anterior insula and anterior cingulate cortex, areas linked to emotional processing and decision-making. This neurological activity strengthens connections and promotes mutual understanding.

Practical Steps to Cultivate Empathy

1. **Active Listening**: Pay full attention to the speaker without interrupting.

2. **Reflect and Validate**: Acknowledge the other person's feelings with phrases like, "That sounds really challenging."

3. **Perspective-Taking**: Try to see the situation from the other person's viewpoint.

Real-Life Story: Healing Through Empathy

When Ravi and Priya faced frequent arguments over parenting styles, they decided to attend a communication workshop. Learning to empathize allowed them to understand each other's fears and intentions, strengthening their relationship and creating a happier home for their children.

Actionable Tip: Practice empathetic listening with a friend or partner this week by focusing on their words without formulating a response until they finish.

Conflict Resolution: Turning Challenges into Growth Opportunities

Why Conflict Happens

Conflict is a natural part of any relationship. It often arises from misaligned expectations, poor communication, or unmet needs.

The Growth Potential in Conflict

Handled constructively, conflict can strengthen relationships by:

- Clarifying misunderstandings.

- Deepening trust through vulnerability.

- Encouraging personal and relational growth.

Steps to Resolve Conflict

1. **Pause and Reflect**: Take a moment to cool off before addressing the issue.

2. **Focus on the Problem, Not the Person**: Use "I" statements instead of blaming, e.g., "I feel frustrated when…"

3. **Seek Win-Win Solutions**: Aim for compromises that meet both parties' needs.

4. **Apologize and Forgive**: A genuine apology and forgiveness are key to healing.

Real-Life Story: Growing Stronger After a Workplace Dispute

Sarah and her colleague James clashed over project responsibilities, leading to weeks of tension. A facilitated discussion helped them uncover their shared goal of team success. By learning to communicate openly, they turned their conflict into a collaborative partnership that benefited the entire team.

Actionable Insight: Approach your next disagreement with curiosity instead of defensiveness. Ask, "What can we learn from this?"

Strengthening Your Social Circle: Strategies for Building Support

The Importance of a Support System

A robust social circle provides emotional support, advice, and shared joy. It also acts as a safety net during challenging times.

Strategies to Build and Maintain Support

1. **Invest in Quality Over Quantity**: Focus on deep, meaningful relationships rather than a large number of acquaintances.

2. **Be Proactive**: Initiate conversations and plan regular meet-ups.

3. **Practice Gratitude**: Show appreciation for the people in your life.

4. **Diversify Your Circle**: Engage with people from different backgrounds to broaden your perspective.

Real-Life Story: The Strength of Friendship in Adversity

After losing his job, Amit leaned on his friend group for emotional and practical support. They helped him polish his resume, connect with job opportunities, and stay motivated. Their support not only eased his transition but also deepened their bond.

Actionable Tip: This week, reach out to one person you haven't spoken to recently and express your gratitude for their presence in your life.

Conclusion: Nurture Connections, Nurture Happiness

Relationships are the heart of happiness. By understanding the science of connection, practicing empathy, resolving conflicts constructively, and strengthening your social network, you can build a fulfilling, joyful life.

Actionable Takeaways

1. Strengthen one relationship by actively practicing empathy.

2. Identify and address a recurring conflict using constructive resolution techniques.

3. Expand your social circle by reconnecting with an old friend or joining a new community.

Happiness thrives in connection. By investing in your relationships, you not only enhance your well-being but also create a ripple effect of positivity that benefits everyone around you.

Resources for Further Reading

1. *The Power of Empathy* by Helen Riess.

2. *The Science of Trust: Emotional Attunement for Couples* by John Gottman.

3. *Nonviolent Communication: A Language of Life* by Marshall Rosenberg.

4. Articles from the Greater Good Science Center at UC Berkeley.

5. Harvard Study of Adult Development (available online for key findings).

Relationships are the bridges to fulfillment. Walk across them with intention and care to find lasting happiness.

CHAPTER 5

CULTIVATING A POSITIVE MINDSET—FROM STRUGGLE TO STRENGTH

"Happiness depends more on the inward disposition of mind than on outward circumstances." – Benjamin Franklin

Introduction: Shaping the Mind for Happiness

Life is full of ups and downs, but your mindset determines whether you grow stronger or feel defeated. Cultivating a positive mindset isn't about denying challenges—it's about learning to navigate them with resilience and optimism. Scientific research has repeatedly shown that a positive outlook can enhance well-being, improve relationships, and even boost physical health.

This chapter dives into the role of optimism, strategies to overcome negativity, the transformative power of a growth mindset, and practical tools like journaling to help you nurture a happier, more fulfilling life.

The Role of Optimism in Happiness

Optimism Defined

Optimism is the expectation of positive outcomes, even in the face of adversity. It's not blind positivity but a realistic confidence that challenges are temporary and manageable.

Scientific Evidence

Research by psychologist Martin Seligman, a pioneer of positive psychology, found that optimistic individuals are more likely to achieve success, maintain better health, and experience greater happiness. Optimism is linked to lower stress levels, enhanced immune function, and reduced risk of chronic diseases.

Real-Life Story: The Optimist's Edge

Samantha, a young entrepreneur, faced repeated failures with her start-up ideas. Instead of giving up, she adopted an optimistic mindset, viewing setbacks as opportunities to learn. Her persistence and belief in eventual success paid off when her third venture became a thriving business. Samantha's story demonstrates how optimism can fuel perseverance and happiness.

Overcoming Negativity Bias: Rewiring for Positivity

What is Negativity Bias?

Negativity bias is the brain's tendency to focus more on negative experiences than positive ones. This evolutionary trait once helped our ancestors survive, but today it often undermines happiness.

The Science Behind It

Neuroscientist Rick Hanson explains that "our brains are like Velcro for negative experiences and Teflon for positive ones." This bias can make setbacks seem overwhelming and obscure the good in life.

Strategies to Overcome Negativity Bias

1. **Gratitude Practices**: Reflecting on things you're thankful for rewires the brain to focus on positives.

2. **Savoring Positive Moments**: Pause to fully experience and appreciate joyful moments.

3. **Reframing Negative Thoughts**: Challenge negative assumptions by asking, "Is this the only possible interpretation?"

Real-Life Story: Finding the Silver Lining

Rajesh, a sales executive, struggled with self-doubt after losing a major client. By practicing gratitude and reframing the situation, he realized the setback was a chance to refine his approach. Within months, his improved strategies earned him even bigger clients, and his renewed positivity made him a happier, more confident leader.

The Growth Mindset: Learning to See Setbacks as Opportunities

Fixed vs. Growth Mindset

Psychologist Carol Dweck's research distinguishes between a fixed mindset (believing abilities are static) and a growth mindset (believing abilities can be developed).

- **Fixed Mindset**: "I'm just not good at this."

- **Growth Mindset**: "I can improve with effort and practice."

How a Growth Mindset Boosts Happiness

People with a growth mindset:

- Embrace challenges as opportunities to learn.

- View failures as stepping stones to success.

- Feel more in control of their happiness and destiny.

Practical Steps to Foster a Growth Mindset

1. **Embrace Challenges**: Seek opportunities to step out of your comfort zone.

2. **Learn from Criticism**: Use feedback as a tool for improvement.

3. **Celebrate Effort, Not Just Results**: Focus on progress, not perfection.

Real-Life Story: A Teacher's Transformation

Anita, a middle school teacher, used to fear technology and avoided integrating it into her teaching. Inspired by a growth mindset workshop, she began experimenting with educational apps. Although she made mistakes initially, her persistence paid off. Her tech-savvy lessons became a hit with students, boosting her confidence and career satisfaction.

Actionable Insight: Choose one area where you feel stuck and approach it with a growth mindset. Replace "I can't" with "I'll learn how."

Journaling and Reflection: Tools for a Happier Mind

Why Journaling Works

Journaling isn't just about venting emotions—it's a scientifically proven tool to enhance well-being. Studies from the University of Texas show that expressive writing helps reduce stress, improve mood, and strengthen resilience.

Benefits of Journaling

1. **Clarifies Thoughts**: Writing helps process emotions and gain perspective.

2. **Tracks Progress**: Seeing growth over time reinforces a sense of accomplishment.

3. **Promotes Gratitude**: Journaling about positive experiences magnifies their impact.

How to Start

1. **Gratitude Journaling**: Write three things you're grateful for daily.

2. **Reflection Prompts**: Use prompts like "What made me happy today?" or "What can I learn from today's challenges?"

3. **Habit Tracker**: Log positive habits to reinforce consistency.

Real-Life Story: Journaling for Clarity

After a difficult breakup, Emily turned to journaling to make sense of her emotions. Over time, her entries shifted from sadness to self-discovery and gratitude. Journaling not only helped her heal but also strengthened her confidence and optimism.

Actionable Tip: Start a 7-day gratitude journaling challenge. Write three positive moments each day and reflect on how they made you feel.

Conclusion: Mindset is the Key to Happiness

Cultivating a positive mindset transforms how you experience life. By embracing optimism, overcoming negativity bias, adopting a growth mindset, and using tools like journaling, you can turn struggles into strengths and setbacks into opportunities for growth.

Actionable Takeaways

1. **Practice Optimism**: Each evening, write down one positive outcome you expect tomorrow.

2. **Reframe Negative Thoughts**: When a setback occurs, ask, "What can I learn from this?"

3. **Journal Daily**: Spend five minutes reflecting on moments of joy and gratitude.

Your mindset is a powerful tool for happiness. Choose positivity, and watch as it reshapes your experiences, relationships, and opportunities for growth.

Resources for Further Reading

1. *Learned Optimism: How to Change Your Mind and Your Life* by Martin Seligman.

2. *Mindset: The New Psychology of Success* by Carol S. Dweck.

3. *Hardwiring Happiness: The New Brain Science of Contentment, Calm, and Confidence* by Rick Hanson.

4. Research papers on gratitude and positivity from the *Journal of Positive Psychology*.

5. Guided journaling apps like Day One and Five Minute Journal.

Happiness isn't found—it's cultivated. Start today, one mindset shift at a time.

ACHIEVING LASTING FULFILLMENT—THE SCIENCE OF PURPOSE

"Efforts and courage are not enough without purpose and direction." – John F. Kennedy

Introduction: Why Purpose is the Key to Fulfillment

In the hustle of everyday life, it's easy to lose sight of what truly matters. We chase fleeting goals, from promotions to possessions, only to find the happiness they bring is temporary. The missing piece? Purpose.

Purpose gives life direction, meaning, and a reason to persevere through challenges. Scientific studies affirm that people who live with a clear sense of purpose report higher levels of happiness, better health, and greater resilience. This chapter explores the transformative power of purpose, how to align values with actions, the magic of flow states, and the profound joy of contributing to something bigger than oneself.

The Role of Purpose in Happiness

Purpose as a Psychological Anchor

Purpose acts as an internal compass, guiding decisions and actions toward meaningful outcomes. It creates a sense of coherence, helping people navigate challenges with clarity.

The Science of Purpose

A landmark study by psychologist Patrick Hill found that having a sense of purpose is associated with lower mortality rates and improved mental health. Purpose reduces stress by fostering a sense of control and direction.

Real-Life Story: A Doctor's Dedication

Dr. Priya Singh, a rural healthcare provider, left a lucrative urban career to serve underprivileged communities. Despite financial sacrifices, she describes her work as deeply fulfilling. "My purpose gives me joy no paycheck ever could," she says. Priya's journey highlights how living with purpose can transcend material rewards.

Aligning Values with Actions: Living Authentically

Understanding Your Core Values

Core values are the principles that matter most to you, such as honesty, compassion, or creativity. Misalignment between values and actions can lead to dissatisfaction and stress.

Bridging the Gap

1. **Identify Your Values**: Reflect on what truly matters to you.

2. **Assess Your Actions**: Evaluate whether your daily choices align with your values.

3. **Adjust and Commit**: Make conscious changes to bring actions in harmony with values.

Example: Living Authentically

Ramesh, a corporate executive, felt unfulfilled despite professional success. Through introspection, he realized his passion lay in environmental conservation. He pivoted to a role in a sustainability-focused organization and found his work aligned with his values, bringing him genuine happiness.

Flow States: The Joy of Being Fully Present

What is Flow?

Flow is the mental state of being completely immersed in an activity, described by psychologist Mihaly Csikszentmihalyi.

It occurs when skill and challenge are perfectly balanced, leading to effortless focus and joy.

Characteristics of Flow

- Time feels distorted (either slowing down or speeding up).

- Focus is intense and distractions fade away.

- The activity feels intrinsically rewarding.

Benefits of Flow for Fulfillment

Research shows that flow enhances creativity, productivity, and overall happiness. It allows individuals to tap into their potential and find joy in the present moment.

Cultivating Flow in Daily Life

1. **Find Your Sweet Spot**: Engage in activities that challenge but don't overwhelm you.

2. **Eliminate Distractions**: Create an environment conducive to deep focus.

3. **Set Clear Goals**: Define objectives for each activity to sustain engagement.

Real-Life Story: The Artist in Flow

Maria, a painter, describes her creative sessions as transcendent. "When I paint, I lose track of time. It's like the world fades away." Maria's experience illustrates how flow can transform routine tasks into sources of profound happiness.

Contributing to Something Bigger: Service and Legacy

The Science of Giving

Helping others is a powerful way to find meaning. Studies from the University of British Columbia show that people who spend money on others or volunteer report greater happiness than those who focus solely on themselves.

The Ripple Effect of Service

When you contribute to your community or a cause, you create a legacy that extends beyond your lifetime. This sense of leaving a mark fosters a deep sense of fulfillment.

Ways to Serve and Build a Legacy

1. **Volunteer**: Dedicate time to a cause that resonates with you.

2. **Mentor**: Share knowledge and experiences to help others grow.

3. **Create**: Build something—art, businesses, or innovations—that benefits others.

Real-Life Story: Leaving a Legacy of Hope

After surviving a life-threatening illness, Jack founded a nonprofit to support patients with similar conditions. "Knowing I'm making a difference gives me purpose every day," he shares. Jack's story exemplifies how service transforms personal challenges into meaningful contributions.

Conclusion: Purpose is the Foundation of Fulfillment

Living with purpose turns life into a journey filled with meaning and joy. By aligning your values with actions, finding flow in daily activities, and contributing to something greater, you can unlock lasting fulfillment.

Actionable Takeaways

1. **Define Your Purpose**: Write down what gives your life meaning and how you can pursue it daily.

2. **Align Values with Actions**: Audit your routine to ensure it reflects your core beliefs.

3. **Create Opportunities for Flow**: Dedicate time to hobbies or work that immerse you fully.

4. **Serve Others**: Find ways to make a positive impact, whether through volunteering or mentorship.

Purpose doesn't just make life worthwhile—it makes it extraordinary. Start small, stay consistent, and watch as your life transforms into a source of joy and inspiration.

Resources for Further Reading

1. *Man's Search for Meaning* by Viktor E. Frankl

2. *Flow: The Psychology of Optimal Experience* by Mihaly Csikszentmihalyi

3. Research articles on purpose and longevity from *Psychological Science*

4. Volunteer opportunities on platforms like VolunteerMatch or Idealist

5. Tools for self-reflection, such as the *Purpose Compass Workbook*

Find your purpose, live your values, and contribute to something bigger—the path to lasting fulfillment begins here.

CONCLUSION: YOUR JOURNEY TO SUSTAINABLE HAPPINESS

"Happiness depends upon ourselves." – Aristotle

Key Takeaways from the Science of Happiness

Over the course of this book, we've delved into the multifaceted nature of happiness and uncovered how science, habits, relationships, and purpose interplay to shape a fulfilling life. Here are the most impactful lessons to carry forward:

1. **Happiness Is a Skill**: Like any skill, it can be culti-vated through intentional effort and practice.

2. **The Role of the Brain**: Understanding the chemistry of joy and leveraging neuroplasticity can rewire our minds for positivity.

3. **The Power of Positive Habits**: Small, consistent actions create lasting change.

4. **The Importance of Relationships**: Genuine connections are central to happiness.

5. **The Purpose Factor**: A sense of direction and alignment with core values enriches life deeply.

6. **Resilience Matters**: Overcoming stress and challenges with the right mindset strengthens mental well-being.

These insights are not abstract theories but practical tools to integrate into your life.

Creating Your Personal Happiness Plan

True happiness requires conscious planning and effort. A well-rounded happiness plan helps you stay committed to your well-being while adapting to life's changes.

Steps to Craft Your Plan:

1. **Set Intentions**: Write down what happiness means to you and why it matters.

2. **Identify Key Areas**: Focus on areas like mental health, relationships, habits, and purpose.

3. **Create Actionable Goals**: Break down goals into daily, weekly, and monthly habits.

4. **Measure Progress**: Use journals, mood trackers, or check-ins to evaluate your journey.

5. **Adjust as Needed**: Flexibility allows you to adapt and grow with new challenges and experiences.

Example: Sarah's Happiness Plan

Sarah, a young professional, built a happiness plan focusing on mindfulness, gratitude journaling, and nurturing her social connections. Over six months, she noticed improvements in her outlook, reduced stress, and deeper relationships.

Commitment to Growth and Well-Being

Happiness is not a destination but a journey that requires ongoing commitment. Growth happens through learning, adapting, and embracing both successes and setbacks.

Tips for Sustained Growth:

- **Stay Curious**: Continuously explore new ideas, practices, and experiences.

- **Practice Self-Compassion**: Be kind to yourself during struggles.

- **Celebrate Wins**: Acknowledge even small progress to stay motivated.

- **Seek Support**: Engage with mentors, friends, or

groups aligned with your happiness goals.

Real-Life Example: Ajay's Resilience

Ajay faced professional burnout but committed to rebuilding his life with mindfulness, regular exercise, and purpose-driven work. His commitment helped him rediscover joy and resilience.

Your Bright Future: Unlocking Fulfillment for a Lifetime

The pursuit of happiness isn't about chasing fleeting pleasures—it's about building a life of meaning, connection, and contentment. By applying the principles in this book, you're taking proactive steps toward a brighter, more fulfilling future.

Final Action Steps:

1. **Revisit Your Purpose**: Reflect on what drives you and how to align your life with it.

2. **Build Resilient Relationships**: Strengthen bonds and practice empathy daily.

3. **Embrace Positive Habits**: Start small, be consistent, and let habits compound.

4. **Find Joy in the Present**: Live mindfully, savoring the beauty of each moment.

Happiness is within reach—it's a practice, a mindset, and a lifelong journey. By committing to growth and prioritizing well-being, you're unlocking a life of sustained joy and fulfillment.

Your Personal Commitment to Happiness

Take a moment to write down:

1. One habit you'll adopt this week.

2. A relationship you'll nurture starting today.

3. One act of gratitude or purpose you'll practice tomorrow.

The choices you make now lay the foundation for your future. Happiness is not just an ideal—it's your reality waiting to unfold. Take the first step and keep moving forward.

Here's to your journey to sustainable happiness—may it be as enriching as it is joyful.

MAY I ASK YOU FOR A SMALL FAVOR?

I want to express my sincere gratitude for choosing to invest your time in reading this book. Your decision to explore this work among countless others means a lot to me.

I hope that within these pages, you've discovered actionable insights that can enhance your daily life. Your journey doesn't have to end here, though.

May I kindly request an additional 30 seconds of your valuable time?

Sharing your thoughts about the book through a review would be immensely appreciated. Your review serves as a beacon, guiding other readers to take a chance on my books. It's a small gesture that carries significant weight in the world of authors.

To submit your review effortlessly, please click on the link below. It will take you directly to the book's review page:

"The Science of Happiness"

Alternatively, you can also find the "**Reviews Section**" of this book's page on Amazon.

Your review will require just a minute of your time but will make a monumental difference in helping me connect with a broader audience and I eagerly look forward to reading your review.

Once again, thank you for your unwavering support of my work.

DISCLAIMER

This book is for educational purposes only. Readers acknowledge that the author does not render legal, financial, medical, or professional advice. The content within this book has been derived from various sources. Please consult a licensed professional before attempting any techniques outlined in this book.

By reading this document, the reader agrees that under no circumstances is the author responsible for any direct or indirect losses incurred as a result of the use of the information contained within this document, including but not limited to errors, omissions, or inaccuracies.

Adherence to all applicable laws and regulations, including international, federal, state, and local governing professional licensing, business practices, advertising, and all other jurisdictions, is the sole responsibility of the purchaser or reader.

Neither the author nor the publisher assumes any responsibility or liability whatsoever on behalf of the purchaser or reader of these materials. Any perceived slight of any individual or organization is purely unintentional.